MW00438917

Especially for

_____

From

_____

Date

_____

Scripture quotations marked NIV are taken from the HOLY BIBLE, NEW INTERNATIONAL VERSION®. NIV®. Copyright © 1973, 1978, 1984, 2010 by Biblica, Inc.™ Used by permission. All rights reserved worldwide.

Scripture quotations marked NLT are taken from the *Holy Bible*, New Living Translation, copyright © 1996, 2004. Used by permission of Tyndale House Publishers, Inc., Wheaton, Illinois 60189, U.S.A. All rights reserved.

Scripture quotations marked MSG are from *THE MESSAGE*. Copyright © by Eugene H. Peterson 1993, 1994, 1995, 1996, 2000, 2001, 2002. Used by permission of NavPress Publishing Group.

Scripture quotations marked NKJV are taken from the New King James Version®. Copyright © 1982 by Thomas Nelson, Inc. Used by permission. All rights reserved.

Published by Barbour Publishing, Inc., P.O. Box 719, Uhrichsville, Ohio 44683, www.barbourbooks.com

Our mission is to publish and distribute inspirational products offering exceptional value and biblical encouragement to the masses.

Member of the
Evangelical Christian
Publishers Association

Printed in China.

Relationship Refreshers

50 Ways to Improve Your Relationship with Your Husband

MariLee Parrish

BARBOUR
PUBLISHING

Contents

To Eric, my best friend. I thank God for the blessing that you are to me, and the wonderful daddy you are to Jake. Even during hard times, you are always "strong, firm, and steadfast."

With special thanks to Pastor Kirt Henman and his wife, Vickie, for being a constant example of an authentic, God-honoring husband and wife. And to Dave and Connie Krizon for all the long talks and orange Kool-Aid during our dating years!

Every marriage needs a lift once in a while. In the pages of this book, we'll seek wisdom from God to find out how we can take your marriage—in whatever condition it's in—and turn it into all that God intends it to be. Some of the items in each reading's "Action Point" and "Checklist for Improvement" can be tackled with your husband if he's a believer. If he's not a believer, ask God to partner with you as you endeavor to refresh your relationship with your spouse.

Second Peter 1:3 says, "His divine power has given us everything we need for a godly life" (NIV), and I believe that includes the power to transform lives and marriages. With Christ as the center of our hearts and homes, anything—and everything—is possible!

Centered on Christ

~Improve Spiritually~

A Fresh Start

For all have sinned and fall short of the glory of God,
and all are justified freely by his grace through
the redemption that came by Christ Jesus.
ROMANS 3:23–24 NIV

Is your marital relationship in need of a little boost? Or maybe even a big boost? We all start out with romantic hopes and dreams, living out life with the man who claimed our heart and praying for that "happily ever after." But then life gets in the way. College loans come due. Children are born. Bodies change. The relationship you started out with can look very different a few years down the aisle. Is there still hope? You bet there is. Through the power of Christ, you have the ability to fall deeper in love with your husband every day. It's time for a fresh start! Spend some time alone in prayer. If you have never asked Jesus Christ to be your personal Savior, take the time and commit your life and your marriage to Him right now. Ask Him to direct your paths and become the Lord of your life. Without His power and love in your life and marriage, there really is no hope. But with Him, He "is able to do immeasurably more than all we ask or imagine" (Ephesians 3:20 NIV)! If you already have a relationship with God, then take your marriage directly to the throne of God.

Heavenly Father, I lift my marriage to You today.
Breathe new life into our union and give us a fresh
start. Open up our hearts to fall in love all over again.
Amen.

Action Point

Commit or recommit yourself to the Lord. Discuss with your husband your desire for a fresh start. If there is unforgiveness in your heart toward one another, start there. Open up to your husband and confess to each other.

Scripture to Remember

Love is patient, love is kind. It does not envy,
it does not boast, it is not proud. It does not dishonor
others, it is not self-seeking, it is not easily angered,
it keeps no record of wrongs.
1 CORINTHIANS 13:4–5 NIV

Checklist for Improvement:

- ❀ If you aren't regularly attending a church, find a Bible-believing congregation and get involved.
- ❀ Write out your wedding vows together and commit to a fresh start.
- ❀ If your husband is a believer, join a couples' Bible study and pray together before you fall asleep each night.
- ❀ Talk to your pastor or a trusted Christian couple about your marriage and your commitment to falling in love all over again. Ask for advice.
- ❀ Visit the church or place you got married.
- ❀ Find old photographs and scrapbooks of when you were dating or newly married. Look through them together.
- ❀ Make a list of things you did or places you visited when you were dating. Make a plan to revisit those places.
- ❀ Get dressed up for your husband on a regular basis—just like you did when you were dating.
- ❀ Take a long walk together. Hold hands.

True and Lasting Change

*If you are a woman with a husband who is not a
believer but he wants to live with you, hold on to
him. . . . God has called us to make the best of it,
as peacefully as we can. You never know, wife:
The way you handle this might bring your husband
not only back to you but to God.*
1 CORINTHIANS 7:13, 15–16 MSG

If your husband is not a believer, then you have an uphill climb. But never forget that many a man has been won over by observing a wife living out an authentic relationship with God. Or maybe your husband is a believer, but his faith is wavering or not very evident in his life—you don't feel like you're on the same page spiritually. This calls for extra prayer and grace. Remember that your husband is God's child first! Only God Himself can make any true and lasting change in your husband's life. That doesn't mean that you enable your spouse to get away with things that aren't acceptable to God. But it does mean that you hand over control of your marriage to the Lord and ask for wisdom when responding to tough situations.

Dear Lord, I pray in Jesus' name that You would draw my husband to You. Soften his heart and give him the desire to follow You. Amen.

Action Point

Commit 1 Thessalonians 5:17–18 (see below) to memory. Then write that scripture reference and the following words on an index card: "True and lasting change comes from God alone. I cannot make anyone change, but I can pray and have a right attitude." Slip this in your Bible or leave it somewhere so that you'll see it daily.

Scripture to Remember

Never stop praying. Be thankful in all circumstances, for this is God's will for you who belong to Christ Jesus.
1 THESSALONIANS 5:17–18 NLT

Checklist for Improvement:

* ❋ Pray for your husband on a daily basis.
* ❋ Ask close friends and women in your Bible study to pray for your husband.
* ❋ Google Charles R. Swindoll's "attitude quote" and post it on your refrigerator.

- ✻ Ask your husband if he would mind if you read a few scriptures together during dinner or before going to bed.
- ✻ Do not force spiritual conversations on your husband. Pray for the right time to bring up the subject of faith, and allow God to lead you.
- ✻ Look for a small group within your church or another Bible-believing church in your neighborhood that is specifically for new believers or those searching for God. Ask your husband to go along.
- ✻ If your husband is uncomfortable attending a small group, ask if he would mind having its members over to your place for dessert and games. He may need to see that the people are normal and personable before he feels open to attending a group.

Centered

"From one man he made all the nations, that they should inhabit the whole earth; and he marked out their appointed times in history and the boundaries of their lands. God did this so that they would seek him and perhaps reach out for him and find him, though he is not far from any one of us. 'For in him we live and move and have our being.' "
ACTS 17:26–28 NIV

$\mathcal{D}$o you keep trying to put God at the top of your to-do list in your marriage? Most of us desire to have God be a part of our marriage in some aspect, but He has so much more planned for us! God wants to be the very center of our lives and marriages—not just at the top of our list of priorities. The Bible tells us that He is not far from each of us. What does that look like in your home? It means that as you cook supper, go to work, spend time with your husband, and go about your day, God is there. He is dwelling within you. You don't have to dial Him up or begin a prayer to summon His power. He is constantly aware of and constantly with you. Understanding that can change the way that you and your husband relate to God. If you want God to be the center of your marriage, remember that He's there—always.

> *I'm amazed that You want to know me and my*
> *husband personally, Father God. You want to be*
> *the very center of our marriage. Thank You for*
> *being with us always. Amen.*

Action Point

Our God is a holy God! But He also wants to have a very personal relationship with each of us. Read Psalm 139. Try committing it to memory. Become more aware that God is constantly present in your life and in your marriage. Allow Him to be the center.

Scripture to Remember

> *"I have called you friends, for everything that I*
> *learned from my Father I have made known to you."*
> JOHN 15:15 NIV

Checklist for Improvement:

❋ Close friendships are based on trust and intimacy. This is true in your relationship with God as well. Even though God already knows your innermost thoughts and feelings, He wants to hear about them from you. Have a heart-to-heart talk with Him today.

❋ Think about what it means to be a good friend to your spouse. Does this apply to your relationship with God? Why or why not?

❋ Talk to God like you would a friend. Begin each day saying "Good morning" to God, just like you do your husband. Then listen for His promptings throughout the day.

❋ Rewrite Psalm 139 in your own words. If your husband is a believer, ask him if he'll do the same. Share your thoughts with each other.

❋ Make a collection of your favorite worship songs that remind you of God's presence. Play them regularly.

❋ Read Deuteronomy 6:5–7. How can you incorporate the message of these verses in your home?

❋ Count your blessings daily. Tell the Lord how thankful you are for each of the blessings in your life.

Remain in the Vine

*"Remain in me, as I also remain in you. No branch
can bear fruit by itself; it must remain in the vine.
Neither can you bear fruit unless you remain in
me. I am the vine; you are the branches. If you
remain in me and I in you, you will bear much
fruit; apart from me you can do nothing."*
JOHN 15:4–5 NIV

John 15:1–17 contains the theme verse of marriage. In fact,
these were the scriptures used at my wedding. We know that
unless we remain in the vine—unless we abide in Christ—we
will not bear fruit in our marriage. God gives us a very clear
picture of what "remaining in Him" looks like. How do we
remain in Him? We obey His command. What is His command? "Love one another as I have loved you" (John 15:12
NKJV). That sums up the entire Word of God in one sentence.
You don't have to memorize a list of rules and regulations.
You don't have to beat yourself up over past mistakes. If you
want your marriage to bear fruit today that will last tomorrow, love each other just as Christ loves you.

*Jesus, help my husand and I to love one another like
You love us. Create fruit in our marriage that will last
throughout the generations. Amen.*

Action Point

Find out if you are loving your husband the way that he needs
you to. You may think are loving him well, but you may be
missing things that are important to him. Ask him what makes
him feel most loved by you, and then put that into action.

Scripture to Remember

> *"If you keep my commands, you will remain in my
> love, just as I have kept my Father's commands and
> remain in his love. I have told you this so that my joy
> may be in you and that your joy may be complete.
> My command is this: Love each other as I have loved you."*
> JOHN 15:10–12 NIV

Checklist for Improvement:

* ❋ Study John 15.
* ❋ Think about your legacy. How can you create
  "fruit that will last" (John 15:16 NIV)? If your
  husband is a believer, discuss this topic with
  him.

- ❀ Purchase a piece of art, or create one yourself, that reminds you of the fruit in John 15.
- ❀ Write down your husband's response when you ask what makes him feel most loved by you. Keep this in your Bible as a daily reminder.
- ❀ Share with your husband what he does that makes you feel most loved.
- ❀ Memorize 1 Peter 4:8.
- ❀ Purchase some fresh grapes for your date night this week as a reminder of remaining in the vine.
- ❀ Tell your husband how much you love him every day. Thank him for being a blessing to you.
- ❀ Write your husband a poem incorporating some of the words from John 15.

Pray

*The earnest prayer of a righteous person has great
power and produces wonderful results.*
JAMES 5:16 NLT

In situations beyond our control, we often hear the phrase "The only thing you can do is pray," which is made to sound like we are resigning ourselves to do next to nothing. Do you have any idea how life-changing a prayer can be? The Bible tells us prayer is powerful and effective. We are also told to approach God's throne with confidence, knowing that we will find the help we need. Every marriage needs prayer. Lots of it! Even if it seems like nothing could shake your relationship, only God knows what is ahead. Any relationship could change for the better or worse in a matter of minutes. So pray continuously. Pray earnestly. Let the power of God do a mighty work in and through you.

*Thank You for allowing us to come boldly into Your
throne room, Lord. Transform us into Your image as
we meet with You each day. Amen.*

Action Point

Commit to approaching God boldly—with all your heart,
mind, body, and soul. Don't just say a quick prayer before
bed, but send up a daily, open, honest prayer about your feelings, your needs, and your circumstances. If your husband is
a believer, commit to praying together as a couple.

Scripture to Remember

*Let us then approach God's throne of grace with
confidence, so that we may receive mercy and find
grace to help us in our time of need.*
HEBREWS 4:16 NIV

Checklist for Improvement:

❄ Plan a daily prayer time. Consider praying
   some prayers out loud.
❄ Eat breakfast with your husband. Pray for him
   before your workdays begin.
❄ If you have children at home, make it a point

to pray with them for your husband while he's at work.

❋ Pray through the Psalms.

❋ Do a search in your Bible about and notate all of the verses that pertain to prayer.

❋ Come before God with a clean heart. If there is any sin in your life that is preventing God from working in you, confess it to Him and repent.

❋ If your husband is a believer, plan a mini prayer retreat. Find a quiet place to go with your spouse. Write down an outline beforehand so you don't get sidetracked, and pray for an hour or two. Try this on a monthly basis.

❋ Pray daily for your husband to resist temptation.

❋ Make a list of your unsaved friends and family. Pray for them regularly.

❋ Pray for ways to share your faith with others.

In the Word

For the word of God is alive and active.
Sharper than any double-edged sword, it penetrates
even to dividing soul and spirit, joints and marrow;
it judges the thoughts and attitudes of the heart.
HEBREWS 4:12 NIV

Are you getting into the Word on a regular basis? If you want to learn to hear God's voice in your life, studying the Bible is a must. God tells us that His Word is "alive and active." That means it has power! As you read the words of the Lord, God uses them to change hearts and circumstances. Isn't that amazing? As you open His Word, you are opening your heart to hear from God. As you read the Bible, you begin to recognize His "still small voice" (1 Kings 19:12 NKJV). If you are wondering if God continues to speak to His children today, He absolutely does! As you memorize scripture and spend more time in God's Word, you will be amazed at how the Holy Spirit brings those verses to your mind at just the right time.

Dear God, give me the desire to be in Your Word.
Give me a thirst that only Your words can quench.
Help me to recognize Your "still small voice"
in my life. Amen.

Action Point

Consider purchasing a Bible study guide that offers discussion questions to help you understand what you're reading in the Word. If your husband is a believer, choose a book of the Bible and read it with him.

Scripture to Remember

I have hidden your word in my heart
that I might not sin against you.
PSALM 119:11 NIV

Checklist for Improvement:

* Start your own or join a Bible study at church.
* Purchase a one-year Bible or make a plan to read through the Bible in a year.
* If your husband is a believer, ask a few other married couples to join you in reading through the Bible in a year. Get together monthly to discuss your results.

* Have a Bible "sword drill" just for fun. Gather the family or your small group. Have a list of scriptures written down. Call out the scripture and say, "Go." The first one to find the verse has to stand up and read it out loud.

* Memorize at least one scripture a week. Don't forget the reference. It's important to know where to find those verses when you need them.

* Many worship songs and hymns come straight out of the Bible. They are scripture set to music. Learn several of them. It's a simple way to memorize God's Word.

* Write down your favorite scriptures or the scriptures you'd like to learn on index cards. Flip through them when you're stuck in traffic or waiting in line.

Devoted

Very early in the morning, while it was still dark,
Jesus got up, left the house and went off
to a solitary place, where he prayed.
MARK 1:35 NIV

To have a healthy marriage, you need to have an individual, healthy relationship with God. Are you devoted to God on a personal level? Your relationship with God should come before anything else: your husband, your children, your family and friends, your work, etc. Nothing matters in life more than an authentic connection with your Creator. We were created to seek Him, find Him, and know Him. No one else can meet all of your needs—not your spouse or any other person or thing or program on this earth. Be devoted to the Lord, and He will fill you with the love and joy you need to be in a healthy relationship with others.

Heavenly Father, You are my Creator and I love You.
Fill me with Your Spirit that I may love You more
and share Your love with those around me. Amen.

Action Point

Start having daily devotions. What does this mean? Carve out time in your day to spend time focusing on God and His Word. Even though God is always with you, you can show your love for Him by reading the Bible, worshipping Him, and praying specifically about your circumstances and the people in your life.

Scripture to Remember

Let the morning bring me word of your unfailing love,
for I have put my trust in you. Show me the way
I should go, for to you I entrust my life.
PSALM 143:8 NIV

Checklist for Improvement:

❋ Set a date with God. Mark it on your planner and meet with God at the same time each day.

❋ Consider getting up a half hour early to meet with God before your day begins.

- ❀ Choose a time of day that works best for you. If you aren't a morning person, make a lunch date with God or find a time when you are at your very best.
- ❀ If your husband is a believer, make sure to share what God is teaching you in your daily devotions.
- ❀ Start a journal chronicling how God is speaking to you during these quiet times.
- ❀ Write a love letter to God in your journal.
- ❀ Read a proverb every day.
- ❀ Ask some trusted friends for their recommendation of a devotional book.
- ❀ See if your church has a library of devotionals you could borrow.

Be Accountable

*Therefore confess your sins to each other and pray
for each other so that you may be healed.*
JAMES 5:16 NIV

Accountability in marriage is a huge deal. Not only should
you be accountable to each other, but each of you should
seek out a strong Christian friend of the same gender whom
you trust. This person should be willing to ask you the tough
questions; and you will need to be willing to give honest an-
swers. This will help strengthen your marriage in many ways.
Having an accountability partner that can help look into
your life and point out the good, the bad, and the ugly will
help you grow closer in your relationship with God and in so
doing will draw you closer to your spouse.

*Bring a strong Christian friend into my life who can
hold me accountable, and help me grow deeper in my
relationship with You, God. I pray that my husband
will find some male accountability partner with
whom he would feel the freedom to be completely open
and honest about his life and relationships. Amen.*

Action Point

Write down a list of your Christian friends. Pray through the
list and ask God to direct you to a person that you would feel
comfortable going deeper with. Make the phone call this week.

Scripture to Remember

> *"For where two or three are gathered together
> in My name, I am there in the midst of them."*
> MATTHEW 18:20 NKJV

Checklist for Improvement:

❋ Set a weekly appointment with your accountability partner and agree that everything
discussed stays between the two of you.

❋ This should be a regular time where you and
your friend share deeply with one another. It

doesn't have to take a lot of time. Consistency and transparency are the keys.

❀ Create a list of questions to ask one another. Here are a few examples:

Have you faithfully served God this week? Why/why not?

Are you spending quality time with God?

Have you been tempted this week?

Are you making your marriage and your family a priority?

Have you acted with integrity this week?

Have you gossiped?

For more ideas visit www.discipleshiptools.org, keyword: accountability questions.

Mentor Moments

Every word you give me is a miracle word—
how could I help but obey? Break open your words,
let the light shine out, let ordinary people
see the meaning.
PSALM 119:129–130 MSG

If you and your spouse have a healthy marriage, it might be time to share your wisdom with others. When my husband and I were going through premarital counseling, our pastor had us do a little research before our wedding day. We were assigned to find a couple who had been married for a number of years and interview them. Find out what works and what doesn't. Hear about the good times and the bad. The couple we interviewed, Dave and Miriam Ramsey, blessed us in so many ways, and they had a major impact in our young married life. Consider volunteering as a mentor in your church. When you become a mentor, you have the opportunity to share the blessings and the knowledge that God has given you with another wife (see Titus 2) or couple just getting started. You might not think you have much to give, but God can work through anyone whose heart is open and yielded to Him.

Dear Lord, show me who needs mentoring.
Give me opportunities to share how You have
blessed and taught me.

Action Point

After praying for direction, call your pastor this week and discuss your willingness to mentor another wife or, if your husband is joining you, an engaged couple.

Scripture to Remember

One generation shall praise Your works to another,
and shall declare Your mighty acts.
PSALM 145:4 NKJV

Checklist for Improvement:

❋ Begin chronicling your married life. Remember the hard times and the times of blessing. Write down how you made it through and what happened.

- ✿ Make a list of the top five things you've learned about marriage.
- ✿ Check out a few books from the library about mentoring.
- ✿ Mentors should have great listening skills and be able to encourage and speak truth into the lives of others. Practice these areas with your spouse.
- ✿ Invite the people you are mentoring over for dinner to let them see your family in action.
- ✿ Ask questions and get to know the people you are mentoring. Don't do all the talking. Let them tell you what they'd like to get out of this mentoring experience.
- ✿ Mentors teach others by being a good example. Allow the people you mentor to be a part of your life.

Marriage on a Mission

*For you have been called to live in freedom,
my brothers and sisters. But don't use your freedom
to satisfy your sinful nature. Instead, use your
freedom to serve one another in love. For the whole
law can be summed up in this one command:
"Love your neighbor as yourself."*
GALATIANS 5:13–14 NLT

Really want to take your marriage to the next level? Serve together! Find a need in your church and fill it—together! You don't have to move to Africa to share God's love with others. And your husband doesn't have to be a believer to help others and find joy in doing so. You can both serve God right where you are—physically and spiritually. Mother Teresa, who spent her life in service to God and others, said: "Prayer in action is love, and love in action is service. Try to give unconditionally whatever a person needs in the moment. The point is to do something, however small, and show you care through your actions by giving your time." Serving will change you. And it will change your marriage, too.

*Heavenly Father, help us live our lives in service to
others. Show us the needs in our church and our
community, and give us the ability to meet them.
Amen.*

Action Point

Call the church secretary and ask about upcoming service
projects or needs in the church. Choose a few things that
you and your spouse can do. Make time in your schedules to
bless others.

Scripture to Remember

*Then Jesus came to them and said, "All authority in
heaven and on earth has been given to me. Therefore
go and make disciples of all nations, baptizing them
in the name of the Father and of the Son and of the
Holy Spirit, and teaching them to obey everything
I have commanded you. And surely I am with you
always, to the very end of the age."*
MATTHEW 28:18–20 NIV

Checklist for Improvement:

✸ Volunteer monthly at a homeless shelter or a
soup kitchen.

- ✻ Make a list of your talents and abilities. How can you use them to bless others?
- ✻ Collect spare change in a jar and give it to someone in need at the end of the year.
- ✻ Consider sponsoring a child through Compassion International.
- ✻ Get involved with Operation Christmas Child (www.samaritanspurse.org) and send a needy child a shoe box full of hope each Christmas.
- ✻ Offer to help clean your church and lighten the load of a custodian or other volunteers.
- ✻ Go on a short- or long-term missions trip together.
- ✻ Volunteer to help with your church's vacation Bible school, or a youth or children's program.
- ✻ Gather clothes and canned goods from friends and family to donate to a homeless shelter.
- ✻ Volunteer with Habitat for Humanity (www.habitat.org) to help build a home for a family in need.

If I allow any turning away from God in my private life, everyone around me suffers.

Oswald Chambers

My Thoughts

....
....
....
....
....
....
....
....
....
....
....
....
....
....
....
....

Connecting the "Knots"

~Improve Emotionally~

Connecting the "Knots"

Though one may be overpowered,
two can defend themselves. A cord of three
strands is not quickly broken.
ECCLESIASTES 4:12 NIV

*U*nderstanding each other emotionally is not an easy task. In an attempt to "connect the knots" and become one with your spouse, you will need God's help. Only your Creator knows you fully. This verse tells us that you and your husband, working as one unit, are more powerful together than you are apart; in addition, a cord of three strands—your husband, you, and God—is even harder to break. Unraveling won't be an issue. God will help you as you try to make sense of emotions in marriage. Two of the most basic human emotions are love and fear. Ask yourself regularly: Am I responding to my husband emotionally out of love or fear? If you and your husband are bound together and Christ is abiding within you, you can always respond out of love.

*Your Word, Lord, tells me that there is no fear in love.
Help me to respond emotionally to my husband out of
the perfect love You have given me. Amen.*

Action Point

Think about the last misunderstanding you had with your husband. Did you respond out of love or fear? Take a moment and analyze the situation. What triggered your response? Should you react differently in the future? Journal your thoughts.

Scripture to Remember

There is no fear in love; but perfect love casts out fear.
1 JOHN 4:18 NKJV

Checklist for Improvement:

❋ When you are tempted to respond out of fear,
   pray for God to change your attitude.

❋ Memorize 1 John 4:18.

❋ If you are prone to negative emotional
   outbursts, take a deep breath before responding
   to your husband and pray for God to take
   control.

* Take a walk, a long bath, or a shower if you have trouble getting your emotions under control.
* If your husband is uncomfortable showing emotion, talk issues through when you are calm and can discuss things without responding negatively.
* When your husband is excited, be excited with him.
* Read Romans 12:15 together. Memorize it. Practice it.

Start Communicating

An honest answer is like a kiss on the lips.
PROVERBS 24:26 NIV

Communication is one of the keys to a healthy emotional relationship in your marriage. One of the first rules of communication is to listen without interrupting. Try to put yourself in your husband's shoes and understand what he is saying. Let him complete his thought, and then honestly share your opinion. Many couples just do not know how to communicate. If your relationship has always been more physical than conversational or if your children seem to get in the way of your communication, it can be very difficult to know where to start. If you have had trouble communicating in the past or if either of you feel uncomfortable expressing yourself, having a list of subjects to talk about is a great place to start.

> *Abba God, we need Your help to communicate*
> *better as a couple. Help us to be open and honest*
> *with each other and with You. Allow us to grow*
> *closer together and to become all that You want*
> *us to be as husband and wife. Amen.*

Action Point

Set a "coffee date" with your spouse. Put the kids to bed a few minutes early and put on a pot of coffee (decaf, if you prefer!). Prepare your husband's favorite dessert. Write out a list of questions for you and your spouse to discuss. If this is your first time, try to keep the list to only about five questions so that this doesn't become overwhelming. Here are a few ideas:

1. Are we where you thought we would be at this stage in our lives?
2. How can I help you feel more loved?
3. Do you feel respected? Why/why not?
4. Is there a goal that I can help you accomplish this year?
5. What do you think we could do to improve our relationship?

Scripture to Remember

> *Do not let any unwholesome talk come out of your mouths, but only what is helpful for building others up according to their needs, that it may benefit those who listen.*
> EPHESIANS 4:29 NIV

Checklist for Improvement:

❀ Plan a coffee date for this week.

❀ Prepare your list of questions, and ask your spouse to do the same.

❀ Purchase or make your husband's favorite dessert in preparation for your coffee date.

❀ If you have children, prepare your children in advance. Let them know that after the bedtime routine, it is time to go to sleep. You won't be going back in for another story or a glass of water. Your coffee date needs to be uninterrupted time with your spouse.

❀ This conversation time with your spouse should be fun. Consider dreaming up a future vacation after you've covered your list of questions.

❀ After your coffee date, write your husband a love note thanking him for the time he spent with you in conversation. Affirm some of the ideas he shared, and tell him how much you look forward to your next date.

❀ Schedule another coffee date for next month—or next week!

❀ If you've had trouble communicating or you are currently experiencing trouble in your marriage, call a truce if at all possible. Commit to sit down and talk it out.

❀ If either you or your spouse is unwilling to sit down and talk, it may be time to see a professional.

Trust Me

For You are my hope, O Lord God;
You are my trust from my youth.
PSALM 71:5 NKJV

Has your husband ever broken your trust? It happens. It will happen—even in the best of marriages. . .even by the most trustworthy spouses. One thing to keep in mind is that people will let you down. Once we put our complete trust in people, we are just setting ourselves up for trouble. People fail us. Jesus never does. God is the only One worthy of our complete trust. This doesn't mean we should live paranoid that our spouse is dishonest or hiding things from us, but it does mean that we accept that our spouse is not perfect. And we aren't either. Your husband is God's child first—and then he's your spouse. We have to trust that God is working in our husbands to make them the men that He intends for them to be as He is working in us to make us the women He intends us to be. Trust God to be the author and sustainer of your husband's life, your own life, and your marriage.

*Lord God, I pray that You would help me trust
You fully and that You would make my husband
strong, firm, and steadfast in his commitment
to You and to our family.*

Action Point

Commit to praying 1 Peter 5:10 for your husband every day.
Write this down in a prominent place so you'll be reminded
to do so!

Scripture to Remember

*And the God of all grace, who called you to his eternal
glory in Christ, after you have suffered a little while,
will himself restore you and make you strong,
firm and steadfast.*
1 PETER 5:10 NIV

Checklist for Improvement:

* Journal your thoughts on trust. Do you put
  more hope and trust in your spouse than you
  do in God?

* Has anyone let you down recently? Forgive him
  or her.

❋ Memorize 1 Peter 5:10.

❋ Every time you think of your husband, pray for him.

❋ Choose to love and forgive your husband on a regular basis. Ask him to do the same for you.

❋ Talk about the importance of trust in a marriage. How should you respond when trust is broken? Journal your discussion.

❋ Let go of the past.

❋ Always tell each other where you've been and where you're going.

❋ If one of you has to work late, call and check in with your spouse every few hours.

❋ Never allow yourselves to be alone with a member of the opposite sex. Discuss ways to avoid this in your marriage.

No Secrets

*Do not lie to each other, since you have taken off
your old self with its practices.*
COLOSSIANS 3:9 NIV

Wanna know the secret to a great marriage? *There are no
secrets* in a great marriage! This verse in Colossians tells all.
Most women would rather be punched in the gut than lied
to. In fact, it feels much the same to us. For many reasons,
you and your spouse may have trouble being 100 percent
open and honest with each other. In all reality, it takes a lot
of practice to learn this kind of marital intimacy. But true,
biblical oneness means that nothing can be off-limits when
it comes to being honest with each other. We live in a society
of deception, where little white lies are the norm. If we take
our marriage vows seriously, we have to learn to go against
the norm.

*Heavenly Father, please forgive me for the little white
lies I've told. Help us to learn to be completely honest
with one another. Amen.*

Action Point

Practice being honest! Our checklist includes a few more
action points to try out immediately with your spouse. Ask
God to convict your hearts when you are not being 100 percent honest or when you tell a little white lie that doesn't seem
to matter.

Scripture to Remember

*What this adds up to, then, is this: no more lies,
no more pretense. Tell your neighbor the truth.
In Christ's body we're all connected to each other, after all.
When you lie to others, you end up lying to yourself.*
EPHESIANS 4:25 MSG

Checklist for Improvement:

❋   Play the "Two Truths and a Lie" game together.
    Come up with two things that are true about
    your day that your husband doesn't already
    know and one thing that isn't true about your

day. Ask your husband to guess which one isn't true. Now it's his turn.

❋ Ask each other why you guessed the way you did. Did you know when the other was lying? Why or why not?

❋ Confess some recent "white lies" to each other. Remember that half-truths are considered deceptions as well.

❋ Talk about why you have lied or told half-truths in the past. Is it so that you won't hurt the other's feelings? Use the examples below to discuss this further:

If your spouse has cooked something awful for dinner and you really don't want him or her to feel bad, but you don't want to lie, and you definitely don't want to *ever* have to eat it again, how can you respond appropriately and honestly in love?

If you buy an outfit that is unflattering and ask for your husband's opinion, how should he respond?

❋ Talk about the difference between brutal honesty and "speaking the truth in love" (Ephesians 4:15 NIV).

❋ Read Proverbs 12.

Walls and Windows

The Lord himself watches over you!
The Lord stands beside you as your protective shade.
PSALM 121:5 NLT

By the time we're married, many of us have become construction professionals. We have learned through years of hurt and heartache how to build walls to protect ourselves. Healthy boundaries are one thing. Concrete walls are another. A pastor and counselor friend of mine, Mike Coen, says that when we build walls to protect ourselves, we are taking God's job away from Him. We have to trust the Lord to be our protector. Mike has also said, "If you do build a wall, make sure to show the other person the window." In other words, if you feel that you need to separate yourself from an emotionally unhealthy person, make sure to show him or her that there are healthy ways to be allowed back in. If you have been hurt emotionally by your spouse, take the steps needed to get healthy. Go see a trusted pastor or counselor, and build a window together.

*You have promised to watch over me, Lord.
Forgive me for the times I try to take my life into my
own hands again. Show me the difference between
building healthy boundaries and building walls.
Amen.*

Action Point

If you are hurting emotionally, make an appointment to see your pastor or a Christian counselor. Ask your husband to join you, even if the problem isn't between you and your spouse. If it is about another friend or family member, your husband can offer his advice and support as well.

Scripture to Remember

*Father to the fatherless, defender of widows—this is God,
whose dwelling is holy. God places the lonely in families;
he sets the prisoners free and gives them joy.*
PSALM 68:5–6 NLT

Checklist for Improvement:

* Purchase and read the book *Boundaries* by
  Henry Cloud and John Townsend.
* Seek out friends and confidants who are mature

believers and good influences on your life.

* Journal your thoughts about boundaries.
* Write down any relationship that feels uncomfortable. Try to analyze why you feel this way.
* Keep your emotions in check. Don't allow them to rule your life.
* Give God daily control of your emotions.
* When choosing a professional counselor or pastor to talk to, make sure you know what the person believes before seeking his or her advice. Look for a counselor who offers sound biblical wisdom.
* Match up everything your counselor tells you with God's Word. If something is contradictory with the Bible, seek a second opinion.
* Today's reading applies to everyday emotional problems in marriages and families, not abusive situations. If you are being abused in any way—emotionally, physically, etc.—seek professional help immediately. This is not something to deal with all by yourself.

Boundaries

> " *For this reason a man will leave his father and mother and be united to his wife, and the two will become one flesh.' So they are no longer two, but one flesh. Therefore what God has joined together, let no one separate.*"
>
> MARK 10:7–9 NIV

*L*et's be straightforward: Some friends or family members may mean trouble for you and your spouse. Their purpose, whether they realize it or not, is to cause division in your marriage. Healthy boundaries are needed to prevent major damage to your marriage from these individuals. Don't let paranoia set in. Most of your friends and family members are supportive and happy to let you live your life. Some, however, say or do things on a regular basis that make you and/or your spouse uncomfortable. These are the people to pray about. Consider creating some necessary boundaries with this person—or persons—to keep you and your spouse from being divided.

Father God, give us wisdom to know how to create
healthy boundaries in our lives, and keep us from
being divided. Amen.

Action Point

Discuss your boundaries with your husband. Talk about scheduling any phone calls (personal or business), family outings, and dinner parties. What time should be just reserved for the two of you? Should family and friends be allowed to come over uninvited anytime, day or night? What you might think is appropriate might not necessarily be okay with your husband. Ask him to share his feelings, then respect them.

Scripture to Remember

You have done many good things for me, Lord,
just as you promised. I believe in your commands;
now teach me good judgment and knowledge.
PSALM 119:65–66 NLT

Checklist for Improvement:

* Discuss family scenarios with your spouse. Talk
  about what is appropriate and what isn't.
* Let everyone in your life know that your
  relationship with your husband is the most

important relationship in your life, other than your relationship with God.

❀ If there are any hard feelings between your husband and your family, call a family meeting to get everything worked out.

❀ Ask parents, friends, and in-laws to call before they stop by your home.

❀ Never make a family boundary decision without your husband.

❀ If you are noticing severe boundary issues within your families, it might be wise to see a professional counselor.

❀ Encourage your husband to take an active role in helping to set family boundaries.

❀ Don't sweep major problems and issues under the rug. Doing so will cause resentment to build up, making the particular issue much worse down the road.

Best Friends

"Greater love has no one than this,
to lay down one's life for one's friends."
JOHN 15:13 NIV

$\mathcal{P}$eter Guiler, a college professor, gave some wise advice to his students: "Find your best friend and marry them." When you are best friends with your spouse, you can get through just about anything. One of the ways to cultivate friendship in your marriage is to treat your spouse as a friend! Be kind and compassionate. Share your day-to-day happenings. Do special things for your spouse just because you were thinking of him. Spend quality time with each other. You don't boss your friends around and expect them to always do things your way, do you? Treat your spouse as a best friend, and he will become one.

*Help me be a better friend to my husband, Lord. Help
us to enjoy each other and our relationship. Amen.*

Action Point

Set aside a weekend day just for you and your husband. With
no major agenda, spend the day together, laughing and sharing your thoughts with each other.

Scripture to Remember

> *Be gentle with one another, sensitive.*
> *Forgive one another as quickly and thoroughly*
> *as God in Christ forgave you.*
> EPHESIANS 4:32 MSG

Checklist for Improvement:

* Pick out a card and small gift for your husband
  this week. Nothing expensive, maybe even just
  a candy bar to let him know you were thinking
  of him.
* Make sure you're always sharing important
  things with your husband first before telling a
  friend.
* Laugh. Giggle. Laugh until you cry.

* Read a wholesome funny story together.
* Laugh about funny things that happened to you when you were young.
* Smile at each other.
* Share your most embarrassing moments.
* Read the comics from the newspaper together.
* Attend a sporting event together.

Syrup or Pasta Sauce?

*Instead, we will speak the truth in love,
growing in every way more and more like Christ,
who is the head of his body, the church.*
EPHESIANS 4:15 NLT

Many wives get frustrated that their husbands don't try to woo them like they did when they were dating. In the book *Men Are Like Waffles, Women Are Like Spaghetti*, Bill and Pam Farrell assert that most men see each element of their lives as a separate compartment or box—like a waffle. Meanwhile women see each element of their lives as touching everything else. To a man, the dating box has been filled, and now you're in the marriage box. To a woman, you're expecting the things you did in your dating years to not only continue, but to be magnified. If you'd like him to continue his courtship of you, you'll have to tell him. Your husband cannot read your mind! That's something to remember forever. Your husband was designed by God to provide, to protect, and to conquer. Most men are project driven and single-minded during that project. Does this sound like your husband? One great thing to realize is that when you do have your husband's complete attention, he is solely focused on you. Once you start to understand this concept and work within God's design, you'll start complementing each other like warm maple syrup on a freshly made waffle.

God, help me to understand my husband better.
I know You created him completely different from me
so that each can complement the other. This was Your
wonderful design. Amen.

Action Point

Think about how your relationship has changed since your dating years. Talk to your husband about this and tell him what aspects you miss. You'll have to be vulnerable here. Asking for flowers or love notes is not an easy thing to do. Speak the truth in love and share from your heart.

Scripture to Remember

And let us consider how we may spur one another on
toward love and good deeds.
HEBREWS 10:24 NIV

Checklist for Improvement:

- ❋ Remind yourself of this daily: "My husband cannot read my mind." Repeat.
- ❋ Try to understand your husband's thoughts and feelings.
- ❋ Try to look at issues from his perspective.
- ❋ If your husband is being insensitive, find a way to talk to him about this without putting him down or being a nag.
- ❋ Share how his actions make you feel instead of casting blame. Say, "When this happens, I feel hurt or confused," instead of "You hurt my feelings all the time."
- ❋ Remove absolutes from your conversations. Avoid these phrases: "You never. . . ," "You always. . ."
- ❋ Praise God for your husband, and thank Him for the qualities He created in him.

Choose Love

Take your everyday, ordinary life—your sleeping,
eating, going-to-work, and walking-around life—
and place it before God as an offering. . . . Fix your
attention on God. You'll be changed from the inside out.
ROMANS 12:1–2 MSG

Love is a choice. Attitude is a choice. You have the option every day to choose love and to choose your attitude. It is your decision. No one else can make it for you. Even if you have been hurt and have a painful past, you can still decide every morning to act out of love for God and others. By fixing all of your attention on God instead of your circumstances, He will bring out the best in you, changing you from the inside out. Most long-time married couples will tell you that they have fallen in and out of love hundreds of times over the course of their marriage. The important thing is to decide to love. No matter what. There will be days when you feel absolutely nothing for your spouse. Choose love. There will be moments when you wish you were anywhere but here.

Choose love. There will be times when you don't want to forgive. Choose love.

Loving Father, give me Your power to choose
love each day. Amen.

Action Point

Decide today that you will never run from your relationship. When you wake up tomorrow morning, begin your day by telling the Lord that you will choose love. Say it out loud.

Scripture to Remember

Above all, love each other deeply,
because love covers over a multitude of sins.
1 PETER 4:8 NIV

Checklist for Improvement:

❋ Take care of any problem while it's small.
❋ Never go to bed angry.
❋ Forgive early and often.
❋ Choose your battles. Overlook the little things.
❋ Protect your marriage. Commit to not let anyone else stir you emotionally except your spouse.

- 🌸 If you have kids, be a good example and provide a solid foundation for them. Show them that your marriage comes first and that you love your husband more than any other person.
- 🌸 Cultivate friendship in your marriage.
- 🌸 Memorize 1 Peter 4:8.

Marriage Checkup

And the peace of God, which transcends all
understanding, will guard your hearts
and your minds in Christ Jesus.
PHILIPPIANS 4:7 NIV

You change the oil in your car every few thousand miles. You go to the dentist regularly for a checkup. How often are you checking on the health of your marriage? As Christians, we must guard our hearts and our marriages. A regular marriage checkup needs to be nonnegotiable. In fact, it is something to look forward to. It's fun to make it a yearly event around your anniversary time: celebrating, sharing, and learning. But it's also a good idea to check your relationship status on a monthly or weekly basis, too. A lot can happen in a year.

I put our marriage in Your hands, Prince of Peace.
Guard and protect it. Show us anything that could
become a problem, and help us work it out. Amen.

Action Point

Plan a weekend getaway for a marriage checkup. Bring your notebooks and Bibles. Spend the weekend discussing your future, your hopes, and your dreams. Pray a lot.

Scripture to Remember

> *Don't go to bed angry. Don't give the*
> *Devil that kind of foothold in your life.*
> EPHESIANS 4:27 MSG

Checklist for Improvement:

Take this advice from several happily married women:

- ❋ "Treat your husband like a king, and he will treat you like a queen" (Andrea Shuler).
- ❋ "Remind each other when you are off the right path. Support each other during the hardest moments. Be objective and honest with each other. If he doesn't look good in a purple shirt, tell him" (Iris Wu).
- ❋ "Laugh together! My husband and I have learned to relax and not take life so seriously all the time" (Jessica Welker-Loveless).

❋ "Think before you speak. Some words/tones can be hurtful. Always be on the same page about raising your children" (Sherry Stanley).

❋ "A couple that laughs together can grow old together—and be totally okay cleaning each other's teeth" (Shara Lawrence-Weiss).

❋ "Always be his number-one fan, and give him a few moments to decompress before dumping or shouting for joy the events of the day" (Merry Lynn Guy).

If your spouse shares your faith. . .

❋ "Be your husband's best friend, lover, and the woman he calls 'baby'! Pray together, laugh lots, and worship the Lord together" (Rhonda Jo Clinton).

❋ "Stay in the Word. It is your guide to a wonderful relationship with your spouse. Study it together, and apply it to your marriage every day" (Beth Aga).

❋ "Whether happy, mad, or sad, sincere and honest praying with your spouse deepens a relationship like nothing else" (Kelly Hohne).

*Find your best friend
and marry them!*

College Professor Peter Guiler

My Thoughts

Where's the Romance?

~Improve Romantically~

Embrace Romance

Enjoy the wife you married as a young man!
Lovely as an angel, beautiful as a rose—
don't ever quit taking delight in her body.
Never take her love for granted!
PROVERBS 5:19–20 MSG

Incorporating romance into your life isn't easy. The honeymoon is over, so adding a little romance in the midst of work, kids, and bills will take effort on both parts. But it can be done, and your marriage will thrive because of it. You may be in a tough spot. You may think that your husband doesn't have a romantic bone left in his body. Just remember that God created romance, and He wants to bless you in this way. He's in the miracle business, and He can find the buried romance bones in your husband's body and get them back in working condition.

*Heavenly Father, thank You for romance. I pray that
You would stir in my heart—and my husband's—a
desire for romantic love again. Amen.*

Action Point

Read the Song of Solomon. Go to www.biblegateway.com
and print portions of it out in several different versions including The Message. If your husband is a believer, take turns
reading it to each other and letting it inspire romance in your
marriage.

Scripture to Remember

*His words are kisses, his kisses words. Everything
about him delights me, thrills me through and
through! That's my lover, that's my man.*
Song of Solomon 5:16 MSG

Checklist for Improvement:

* Purchase *Simply Romantic Nights*. You can find
it online or at your local Christian bookstore. It
is full of scriptural thoughts and ideas to keep
the fire burning in your marriage.

* Consider renewing your vows. If not in front of
a crowd, repeat them to each other in a special

private ceremony. Then let the honeymoon
begin all over again.

❀ Go to the fragrance counter at a department
store together. Pick out new scents for each
other to try.

❀ Light the candles over dinner.

❀ Pick out some new romantic music together.

❀ During intimacy, think only of your husband,
not everything else on your to-do list.

❀ Make time for intimacy. Don't schedule
activities for every night of the week. Respect
each other's time.

❀ Plan regular bubble baths with candles and soft
music.

It's a Date

Oh, lover and beloved, eat and drink!
Yes, drink deeply of your love!
SONG OF SOLOMON 5:1 NLT

Every married couple needs a weekly date night. It doesn't have to be expensive, and you don't even have to leave the house! But it does need to be regular and nonnegotiable. If you can't afford to go out often, plan fun dates at home or pack a lunch and go on a picnic within walking distance. The point is to set a scheduled time each week to focus on each other without any other distractions. Watching a movie together at home is nice and relaxing, but to count as a date night, some conversation and focused attention must take place. If you already watch a movie together each week, just plan on adding coffee and dessert after it's over. During the dessert you can discuss your thoughts about the movie and share more deeply with each other.

Help us to make each other a priority, Lord God.
Thank You for date nights. Allow us to build intimacy
during these times. Amen.

Action Point

Get your calendars out and schedule a weekly date night. Add it to your budget if you can. Several inexpensive ideas are listed below. If a night out once a week simply won't work in your budget, try for once a month. But remember, a weekly date night isn't optional. You can date each other without leaving home!

Scripture to Remember

I am my lover's, and my lover is mine.
SONG OF SOLOMON 6:3 NLT

Checklist for Improvement:

* ❁ Play a game of chess or checkers together.
* ❁ Go on a quarter date. Exchange some cash for a roll of quarters. Pay only with quarters everywhere you go, and see how far it will take you. Buy a burger at one place, dessert at the next, and finish with a few games at an arcade.

- ❀ Wash the car together. Spray each other down. Flirt a little. Flirt a lot.
- ❀ Take your car to an automatic car wash. Steam up the windows from the inside.
- ❀ Plan a scavenger hunt for the two of you.
- ❀ Make your husband breakfast in bed.
- ❀ Take turns giving each other massages.
- ❀ Plan a French, Italian, or Mexican theme night. Cook dinner, watch a movie, do an activity all related to that theme.
- ❀ Go on a romantic drive together at dusk. Watch the sunset.
- ❀ Go see a drive-in movie. Bring blankets for cuddling.

Full House

I belong to my beloved, and his desire is for me.
SONG OF SOLOMON 7:10 NIV

Romance with young kids in the house takes extra effort. Many times it is too expensive to hire a sitter for a weekly night out, so many of your dates will have to occur at home where you can still have a romantic evening—with a little practice. Put the kids to bed early one night a week and add a little ambience to the family room or bedroom. Make sure to freshen up and look your best, just like you did when you were dating. Plan some topics to discuss, prepare a favorite dessert, or use some of the ideas listed in this book. Having a full house doesn't have to stifle your romance; you just have to learn to work with what you've got. Remember, the kids won't be little forever. This is just a season of life that will be over before you know it. You may even wish for it back! So cherish this time of crayon drawings and sloppy kisses—and find ways to cherish each other amid the sleepless nights and toy-strewn rooms.

Lord, romance in our marriage is very important to me. Thank You for our little ones, but please give us the time and energy to focus on our relationship, too.

Action Point

Research fun date-night activities that can be done at home. Make a list and put them on the calendar for the next few months. Do something different each week until you get to the end of your list. Then start over or do some more research.

Scripture to Remember

Place me like a seal over your heart, like a seal on your arm; for love is as strong as death, its jealousy unyielding as the grave. It burns like blazing fire, like a mighty flame.
SONG OF SOLOMON 8:6 NIV

Checklist for Improvement:

❋ Finding energy to be romantic after the kids are in bed can be difficult. Be careful to keep yourself healthy.

❋ Take a daily vitamin.

❋ Make sure you are getting enough rest. Rest

when the kids are resting.

- ❃ Exercise regularly. Exercise with the kids.
- ❃ Purchase candles and soft pillows to help transform your family room or bedroom.
- ❃ Talk about expectations with your spouse. After a long day with young kids, a night of romance is unlikely. Plan your date night on a weekend when you have more help during the day and a time to rest.
- ❃ Trade babysitting on a monthly basis with another couple from church who has young children.
- ❃ Be affectionate with your spouse regularly—in front of your children. Hold hands and let them see you hug and smooch every now and then, too.

Got No Money, Honey!

Keep your lives free from the love of money and be content with what you have, because God has said, "Never will I leave you; never will I forsake you."
HEBREWS 13:5 NIV

Romance doesn't have to be expensive. Sure, having plenty of money makes romance easier, but that takes some of the magic out of it. Isn't it extra special to find out that your husband has saved up to buy you that gift or bring you some flowers? Perhaps it pleases you to buy your husband a little something. God's Word tells us to be content with what we have. He promises never to forsake us, and He knows that you and your husband need romance in your marriage. Trust Him to take care of you and to provide. While having an expensive dinner and night out every so often can be a wonderful thing if you can afford it, you can accomplish the same romantic results with a whole lot less.

*Jesus, help me to be content with our financial
situation, and give us creative ideas to make romance
work with what we can afford. Amen.*

Action Point

If receiving a gift or flowers every now and then from your
husband is important to you, add a small mystery fund to
your budget. Pull out just a few dollars from every paycheck,
and your husband can stash it away to use as he sees fit.

Scripture to Remember

*I know what it is to be in need, and I know what it
is to have plenty. I have learned the secret of being
content in any and every situation, whether well fed
or hungry, whether living in plenty or in want.*
PHILIPPIANS 4:12 NIV

Checklist for Improvement:

* ❋ Visit the dollar store and purchase candles to
  use for romantic evenings at home.
* ❋ Go stargazing. Pick out the constellations.
* ❋ Have an indoor picnic in front of the fireplace.
* ❋ Play a video game together. The loser has to
  make the winner dinner.

- ❀ Go to a local coffeehouse when live music is playing. Spring for a few cups of coffee, and you're set.
- ❀ Go ice-skating. Take a thermos of hot chocolate with you.
- ❀ Go to the bookstore. Pick out a devotional book to read together.
- ❀ Join a book club together.
- ❀ Visit a chocolate or cheese factory. Take a tour and enjoy some free samples.
- ❀ Organize a progressive dinner with several of your friends. Appetizer at one couple's house, dinner at another, dessert at the final destination.

25

Fall in Love Again. . . Every Day

Many waters cannot quench love;
rivers cannot sweep it away.
SONG OF SOLOMON 8:7 NIV

If you have been married for a while, the spark may be gone from your eyes. The butterflies in your stomach have likely flown away, and you've begun to see your husband as a roommate instead of the man who swept you off your feet. Is there hope for your marriage? A resounding yes! The first thing you should do is pray for change. But the second thing might take some convincing. Christian author John Maxwell says, "You need to act your way into feeling." Sounds a little dishonest, doesn't it? But think about it for a minute: Your relationship with God should be based on truth, not on what you feel. Some days we don't feel very close to God, right? But we still choose to love Him and believe He's there. It's the same in marriage. If you don't feel like you're still in love with your spouse, tell yourself that you are and treat him with love and respect. Pretty soon he'll start doing the same with you.

Heavenly Father, I don't feel very in love with my husband right now. Please change my heart and help me to treat him as I should. Amen.

Action Point

Spend the next ten days consciously treating your husband with love and respect using your own ideas or the ones listed below. At the end of the ten days, evaluate any changes that have taken place. Then keep plugging away, no matter what. God is working in your marriage even if you can't see it right now.

Scripture to Remember

Now that you've cleaned up your lives by following the truth, love one another as if your lives depended on it.
1 PETER 1:22 MSG

Checklist for Improvement:

❋ Send your husband a love note at work.

❋ Meet him at the door with his favorite snack when he gets home from work.

- ❀ Ask a friend to watch the kids for an hour. Then pack a picnic lunch and meet him on his lunch break this week.
- ❀ Tell him how much you appreciate how he has provided for you and your family.
- ❀ Visit a museum together.
- ❀ Go to the zoo or an amusement park.
- ❀ Skip through the park together.
- ❀ Go see a wholesome romantic movie, then to a coffee shop afterward to talk.
- ❀ Have a snowball fight. No snow? Use pillows.
- ❀ Go bowling.

26

The Love Tank

My beloved friends, let us continue to love each other since love comes from God.
1 JOHN 4:7 MSG

Do you know your husband's love language? Dr. Gary Chapman suggests that there are five main love languages that people need to feel loved. If you are not speaking your husband's love language, his love tank will be on empty. And the opposite is also true. Go back through your married life in your mind and think about the times when your husband was most content, happy, and responsive. Was it when you were telling him how much you appreciate him? Was he receiving a gift? Were you doing something special with him or for him? It is essential to find out when your husband feels most loved by you. And vice versa. It could make all the difference.

Lord God, give us wisdom to know how to love each other correctly. Amen.

Action Point

Purchase *The Five Love Languages* by Dr. Gary Chapman and begin reading it as a couple. Consider hosting a small group to discuss this book and share what God has been teaching you.

Scripture to Remember

> *Don't just pretend to love others. Really love them.*
> ROMANS 12:9 NLT

Checklist for Improvement:

* Go to www.5lovelanguages.com and take a quiz to find out your and your love language.

* Is his love language "affirming words"? If so, make sure you're telling him how much you love and appreciate him daily.

* Does quality time fill his tank? If so, make sure you aren't too busy to spend regular, lengthy amounts of time with him.

* Is physical touch how he feels most loved? Then be available and willing to love him the way he needs.

- ❀ If your husband appreciates it when you do things for him to ease his responsibility, make sure the house is cleaned up, offer to help with a difficult work assignment or chore, or offer to clean his car.
- ❀ If receiving gifts is his primary love language, make a list of his favorite things from least expensive to most expensive. Purchase them as you can afford to.
- ❀ Make him a practical, homemade gift.

Words of Love

*So this is my prayer: that your love will flourish
and that you will not only love much but well.*
PHILIPPIANS 1:9 MSG

Your husband needs to hear how much you love and respect him. Even if you show him in countless ways, it's important that he hear the words. Yes, actions always speak louder than words. But when you are showing him that you love him and those actions are backed by words spoken straight from your heart, your husband will be a happy man. Some of us have a hard time verbally making our feelings known. While this can be overcome with a little practice, a written note works well, too.

*Abba God, I pray that You would allow our
love to flourish. Let us fall more in love
with each other every day.*

Action Point

We are busy women, and we can easily forget to do these small things that can mean so much to our husbands. Place a reminder on your calendar a few times a month to write your husband an encouraging note or send him an e-mail at work, telling him how much you love and appreciate him.

Scripture to Remember

> *I thank my God every time I remember you. . . .*
> *It is right for me to feel this way about all of you,*
> *since I have you in my heart.*
> PHILIPPIANS 1:3, 7 NIV

Checklist for Improvement:

* Pack your husband's lunch a few times a week. Slip a love note in along with his favorite snack.
* Send your husband an e-mail a few times a month, reminding him that you love him and/ or letting him know that you've prayed for him today.
* Have your kids create cards a few times a month to slip into his lunch or place on the driver's seat of his car.

❀ After your husband leaves the office, call his work phone and leave him a voice mail, thanking him for working so hard for you and your family. Receiving this first thing in the morning will get his day off to a great start.

❀ Leave a love note under his pillow, telling him how handsome he is.

❀ Create a heart-shaped note and slip it into his shoes.

❀ If your husband leaves for work before you wake up, write him a note (in lipstick) on your bathroom mirror before you go to bed.

Love's Power

*It always protects, always trusts, always hopes,
always perseveres. Love never fails.*
1 CORINTHIANS 13:7–8 NIV

Love never fails." That is a powerful statement. I'll never forget a sermon I heard years ago. Our pastor at the time, Rev.
Ralph Wiley (who has since gone home to be with his Savior
and wife of fifty-nine years) said that if a man is happy in his
marriage, not much else in the world can get him down. Not
the loss of a job, not his past, not any of his circumstances.
If his wife is loving, respectful, and supportive, that man can
get through just about anything! Commit to being that kind
of wife. Ask the Lord for His blessing on your marriage, and
allow His love to pour through you in powerful ways that can
change the heart of your husband—and the atmosphere of
your home. Love is a powerful thing.

*Lord, I pray that You would bless our marriage
and that Your love would be evident in my life
and in my home. Amen.*

Action Point

Talk about your relationship with your spouse. Share your heart and listen to his. Ask him how you can better support, respect, and love him.

Scripture to Remember

*And now these three remain: faith, hope and love.
But the greatest of these is love.*
1 CORINTHIANS 13:13 NIV

Checklist for Improvement:

* ❋ Tell him you love him. Show him you love him.
* ❋ Tell him you like him. Show him you like him.
* ❋ Don't nag. If you don't feel like your husband is paying attention, talk to him honestly about how this affects you.
* ❋ "Let go of the small stuff. We all have annoying habits and preferences that are different from our spouse's" (Dave Ramsey).

* Be kind and loving to your husband. Treat him how you would like to be treated.
* Give him a true day off every once in a while.
* Show interest in his friends and hobbies.
* Don't argue with or disrespect your husband in public or in front of your children.
* Ask for his advice on a regular basis. Let him know you appreciate his opinion.

A Love Affair

*Follow God's example, therefore, as dearly loved
children and walk in the way of love, just as Christ
loved us and gave himself up for us as a fragrant
offering and sacrifice to God.*

Ephesians 5:1–2 niv

God wants you and your spouse to share a deep love affair all the days of your life. "Till death do you part." God's Word tells us that we can stand firm in Christ and that He has set His Spirit in our hearts (see 2 Corinthians 1:21–22). We have the power of Christ living in us to love one another just as God has loved us. Be encouraged. What may seem like a loveless marriage can be completely transformed into one that honors the Lord. The power of God is available to you because of what Jesus Christ did for us on the cross. He is living today, and He is working in your life and in your marriage. The love that you and your husband share can leave a legacy for all those that come after you, pointing others to the Author of love and giving Him glory!

*I know You, Lord, are able to do much more than I
can hope or imagine. Allow our love affair to point
others to You. Amen.*

Action Point

Look into your husband's eyes and tell him that you are deeply
in love with him.

Scripture to Remember

*What is clearest to me is the way Christ treats the church.
And this provides a good picture of how each husband
is to treat his wife, loving himself in loving her,
and how each wife is to honor her husband.*
EPHESIANS 5:32–33 MSG

Checklist for Improvement:

❋ Always say encouraging and respectful things
   about your husband in public. Let him
   overhear you on occasion.

❋ If you have children, tell them often how much
   you love their dad.

❋ Have pizza delivered to your husband's place of
   employment, and send an encouraging note if

your husband needs to work late one night.

❋ Let your husband know that he comes first in your life, before any other human relationship.

❋ Sign up for a daily devotional at www.familylife.com; romance tips are included.

❋ Plan a surprise weekend getaway.

❋ Flowers don't have to be for women only—buy a single red rose and attach a love note letting him know you're thinking about him.

❋ Plan a treasure hunt around your house or neighborhood just for your husband. Let the clues lead to a special gift—or you!

Celebrate!

"I have come that they may have life,
and have it to the full."
JOHN 10:10 NIV

Your marriage is something to celebrate. Don't let your anniversary slip by each year without taking time to thank God for each other and enjoying one another! Do something different this year. If you normally plan the annual dinner out for your anniversary, try a weekend getaway. If you normally plan a weekend away, consider renewing your vows in front of friends and family. Whatever you decide on, make it monumental. It is no small thing that you have been given these years together. If you are healthy and happy, earnestly thank the Lord for such blessings. If you are struggling through a rough patch, pray for God's healing. With lives and marriages crumbling all around us, it's important to be thankful and count your blessings together. Celebrate your marriage. Celebrate God's goodness.

*Lord of Creation, thank You for providing a helpmate
for me. Thank You for another year together. May we
always be filled with Your joy. Amen.*

Action Point

Go all-out this year. Call the travel agent and start saving for
a special trip with your husband. If you can't afford anything
too extravagant, do the best you can with what you have and
keep putting money away for the next big milestone.

Scripture to Remember

*They tell of the power of your awesome works—
and I will proclaim your great deeds. They celebrate
your abundant goodness and joyfully sing of your
righteousness.*
PSALM 145:6–7 NIV

Checklist for Improvement:

* ❋ Schedule a marriage retreat. Check out
  www.familylife.com.
* ❋ Print out your vows in a beautiful font. Have
  them framed and hang them above your bed.
  Place his vows on your side, and your vows on his.

- 🌸 Send a special gift to him at work.
- 🌸 Make a special coupon book just for your husband.
- 🌸 Write a love poem telling your husband how much you appreciate and respect him.
- 🌸 Put together a basket of your husband's favorite snacks and treats. Present them to him on your anniversary trip.
- 🌸 Have silly photos taken together in a mall photo booth.
- 🌸 Sleep in and spend the day cuddling.

A happy marriage is the union of two good forgivers.

Ruth Bell Graham

My Thoughts

....

....

....

....

....

....

....

....

....

....

....

....

....

....

A Healthy Heart

~Improve Physically~

After the Wedding

Don't you realize that your body is the temple of the Holy Spirit, who lives in you and was given to you by God? You do not belong to yourself, for God bought you with a high price. So you must honor God with your body.

1 CORINTHIANS 6:19–20 NLT

We've all seen what happens after the wedding. Maybe not to us—but to "that other couple." The husband has won the heart of his princess. The princess feels secure in her man's arms. Everyone starts getting comfortable. Regular workouts take a backseat. Takeout and local restaurants become the norm. The stretchy pants come out of the closet, and before you know it, there are a few more pounds here and a few more pounds there. This doesn't happen to everyone, but it does happen a lot. The danger is that a few years down the road, you'll wake up next to a person whom you've never seen before. Not to mention you're putting your own health in jeopardy. This not-to-be-overlooked section of the book will focus on keeping your heart healthy for the sake of your marriage.

*God, please help us not to take advantage of what
You've given us. Strengthen our marriage by helping
us be good stewards of our health. Amen.*

Action Point

Sit down with your spouse and have a serious discussion about your health. Affirm to him that you still find him attractive. Explain that both his and your own health need to take a more prominent role in your home.

Scripture to Remember

*And so, dear brothers and sisters, I plead with you to give
your bodies to God because of all he has done for you.
Let them be a living and holy sacrifice—
the kind he will find acceptable.*
ROMANS 12:1 NLT

Checklist for Improvement:

* ❋ Join a health club together.
* ❋ Go on a walk together every night after dinner.
* ❋ Cook a healthy meal together at least once a week.

- ❄ Decrease the frequency of your meals out. Cook healthy meals at home instead.
- ❄ Pack your lunches.
- ❄ Eliminate white flour and processed foods from your diet.
- ❄ Eat an apple every day.
- ❄ Avoid all fast-food. Order a salad with low-fat dressing, or head to a sandwich shop where you can order lean meat, veggies, and whole grain bread if you absolutely must get something on the go.
- ❄ Fill your grocery cart with more fruits and veggies.
- ❄ Eat your meals slowly, and stop when you're full.

Change of Heart

A peaceful heart leads to a healthy body;
jealousy is like cancer in the bones.
PROVERBS 14:30 NLT

The way you treat your body affects every area of your life. It is a scientific fact that stress can cause major medical problems. Even the Bible says that a heart at peace leads to a healthy body. It can't be ignored. If you are treating your body with disrespect it will negatively affect your health, your marriage, and your whole life. Maybe a complete overhaul is needed in your marriage, but a slow and steady change will make a world of difference, too. Taking everyday steps in the right direction will lead to long-term success.

Heavenly Father, help me to make better choices when
it comes to my health so that I may honor You and my
husband with my body. Amen.

Action Point

Start planning healthy meals. Create a weekly meal plan and grocery list. Exchange pre-packaged and high-calorie snacks for healthier options.

Scripture to Remember

"I will always show you where to go. I'll give you a full life in the emptiest of places—firm muscles, strong bones. You'll be like a well-watered garden, a gurgling spring that never runs dry."
ISAIAH 58:11 MSG

Checklist for Improvement:

* Visit www.e-mealz.com to find healthy meal plans. They also provide a grocery list using prices from the grocery stores you frequent to help you stick to your budget.
* Start reading the labels on the packaged foods you buy. Avoid items with high sodium, hard-to-pronounce names, preservatives, and trans fats.
* Forego the meat and eat a vegetarian meal at least once a week.

- ✽ Drink at least two quarts of water a day.
- ✽ Limit your caffeine intake to one cup a day.
- ✽ Eat yogurt or take acidophilus on a regular basis.
- ✽ Every morning eat breakfast with plenty of whole grains.
- ✽ Eat a healthy snack when you feel hungry.
- ✽ Don't eat before bedtime. If you need a late-night snack, try an instant breakfast drink with milk.
- ✽ Switch to low-fat milk and cheese.

Keep It Fun

A cheerful disposition is good for your health;
gloom and doom leave you bone-tired.
PROVERBS 17:22 MSG

Living a healthy lifestyle can be great fun! If you and your husband commit to getting fit together, you'll not only improve your health but also your marriage. When you cook together and work out together, not only do you build intimacy but you're able to challenge each other in fun ways. Going through this together is much more enjoyable and rewarding than going it alone. Below are some fun ideas for getting fit that won't feel much like exercise. Enjoy yourself!

Give us the right attitude for getting fit, Lord.
Allow us to enjoy ourselves while we strive to keep
our bodies healthy. Amen.

Action Point

Challenge each other to a contest. Decide what you'd like to accomplish (losing the most weight, running the farthest, doing the most crunches, etc.) and come up with a fantastic prize for the winner.

Scripture to Remember

Why is everyone hungry for more? "More, more," they say.
"More, more." I have God's more-than-enough,
more joy in one ordinary day.
PSALM 4:7 MSG

Checklist for Improvement:

- ❀ Go hiking.
- ❀ Jump rope.
- ❀ Take a workout class together.
- ❀ Hula-Hoop together.
- ❀ Read a book or watch a good movie while riding your stationary bike.

- Walk briskly at the mall.
- Play tennis.
- Plant a garden together.
- Ride bikes.
- Play Ping-Pong.

Accountability Works

*Two are better than one, because they have a good
return for their labor.*
ECCLESIASTES 4:9 NIV

You have a better chance of getting healthy together than you do on your own. Even if your spouse isn't ready to commit to a lifestyle change just yet, you can still find a friend to hold you accountable and work out with you. If you and your spouse are both healthy and active, it's still a good idea to find a walking partner among your friends. Instead of meeting for coffee once a week, go for a nice walk in the park when it's warm and around the mall when it's cold. Share your fitness goals with your friend and ask her to check in on you to make sure you're staying on track.

Father God, put someone in my life to hold me
accountable to follow Your ways and strive to
live a healthier lifestyle. Amen.

Action Point

Ask your husband if he is willing to be your fitness accountability partner. Talk about your goals, and ask him to share
his goals with you.

Scripture to Remember

Carry each other's burdens, and in this way
you will fulfill the law of Christ.
GALATIANS 6:2 NIV

Checklist for Improvement:

❋ Memorize five extra scripture verses as you
   work out this week.
❋ Share your week's menu with your
   accountability partner.
❋ Go grocery shopping with your accountability
   partner.
❋ Share your weight loss progress with your
   accountability partner.

- ❀ Join an aerobics class together.
- ❀ Don't be offended or discouraged if your accountability partner gets on your case about your goals. That's what she's there for.
- ❀ Be willing to listen to constructive criticism.

It's Okay to Cheat

*These liars have lied so well and for so long that
they've lost their capacity for truth. They will tell
you not to get married. They'll tell you not to eat
this or that food—perfectly good food God created
to be eaten heartily and with thanksgiving by
believers who know better! Everything God created
is good, and to be received with thanks.*

1 Timothy 4:2–4 msg

Did you really just read, "It's okay to cheat," in a book about
marriage? We're just talking about food here, folks. If you put
yourself on such a strict diet with no wiggle room at all, you
are sure to fail. Cut yourself some slack every so often and
allow yourself a treat. Reward yourself for good behavior. All
foods can be enjoyed in moderation every once in a while.
If you are worried that you'll eat the entire cake, stop by the
bakery and order just one slice instead. Consider walking to
the ice cream shop and back if your sweet tooth is really kicking in. If you're going to cheat a little, make sure you have

proper boundaries and accountability in your life to keep you from falling off the wagon permanently.

Lord, thank You for all the wonderful foods You've permitted us to enjoy. Help me to enjoy them in moderation. Amen.

Action Point

Make Friday nights your "Cheat Night." Spring for pizza and soda, followed by chocolate and a movie with your sweetheart. This gives you something to look forward to every week.

Scripture to Remember

"I have the right to do anything," you say— but not everything is beneficial. "I have the right to do anything"—but not everything is constructive.
1 CORINTHIANS 10:23 NIV

Checklist for Improvement:

* ❋ Make a batch of cookies. Reserve a few to enjoy on Friday night. Freeze the rest for later.
* ❋ Make your own pizza using turkey pepperoni.

- ❀ Exchange milk chocolate for dark chocolate.
- ❀ Swap the chips for popcorn.
- ❀ Sugar-free pudding with low-fat whipped topping makes a great dessert.
- ❀ Avoid sweets with high-fructose corn syrup.
- ❀ Switch to low-fat ice cream.
- ❀ Try chips and nachos that are baked instead of fried.
- ❀ Make your own desserts. Share the leftovers with a friend or neighbor.
- ❀ Count out sweets and treats into 100-calorie portions. Package them in individual baggies.

36

Rest

By the seventh day God had finished the work he had been doing; so on the seventh day he rested from all his work. Then God blessed the seventh day and made it holy, because on it he rested from all the work of creating that he had done.

GENESIS 2:2–3 NIV

Are you getting enough rest? We're not just talking about those precious eight hours at night, but a true rest from the strains of life. In today's society, weekends are filled with sports, extra jobs, housework, school activities, and more. God created rest for a purpose: to quiet ourselves and have fellowship with Him and to refuel for the coming week. Give yourself one day a week where you do nothing but rest from activities and work. Leave your laptop alone and shut off your phone if you must. Use this day to spend quality time with God and your family. It's been said, "If you burn the candle at both ends, you aren't as bright as you think you are." Take that to heart. Severe burnout can lead to unhealthy lives and even unhealthier marriages.

*Help me realize that my work is not more important
than Yours, God. You rested, and so should I. Amen.*

Action Point

Do nothing. That's right. Today's action point is to rest. Shut
out the world and focus on God and family. Stay in your pa-
jamas and enjoy each other as a couple and/or family.

Scripture to Remember

*"Come to me, all you who are weary and burdened,
and I will give you rest."*
MATTHEW 11:28 NIV

Checklist for Improvement:

- ❋ Before resting, avoid snacks that will raise your
  blood sugar.
- ❋ Turn the TV off and enjoy some silence.
- ❋ Go to the backyard or drive to a nearby park
  and listen to the sounds of God's creation.
- ❋ Your body manufactures Vitamin D when
  you're exposed to the sun's rays. So to obtain
  that essential nutrient, sit in the sunlight for at
  least five minutes a day.

* Read soothing scripture and pray before going to bed.
* Memorize Romans 15:13. Say it aloud before going to sleep at night.
* Focus on positive things before taking a nap or going to bed.
* Keep a notebook by your bed. On those nights when you are lying awake in bed, write down your thoughts and get them out of your head.
* Take a warm bath or shower before resting.

Stress-Less

*You will keep in perfect peace those whose minds
are steadfast, because they trust in you.*
ISAIAH 26:3 NIV

Stress is a killer. It is the enemy of healthy living and the downfall of many a marriage. It is a scientific fact that stress can cause major health issues. So what do we do? Our world is full of stress and anxiety-causing issues. We can't avoid that. However, as Christians we have a solution! The Bible promises that in this world we will have trouble (see John 16:33), but we are to trust that God is in control. When you are in the middle of a crisis and stress is causing issues in your life and marriage, cast your anxiety on the Lord. Ask Him to remove the anxiety you are feeling and help you manage it. It has been said by many in a variety of ways that true peace isn't the absence of trouble—it's the presence of God in the midst of trouble.

*Heavenly Father, I trust that You are aware of
how I'm feeling. Give me the peace that passes
understanding as You walk me through this. Amen.*

Action Point

Make a list of all of the stresses and problems in your life that
are causing you anxiety. One by one, lift them up in prayer to
the Lord and cast those burdens onto Him.

Scripture to Remember

> *Cast all your anxiety on him because he cares for you.*
> 1 PETER 5:7 NIV

Checklist for Improvement:

* ❊ Keep a journal of scriptures to repeat and pray
  over when feeling stressed.
* ❊ Memorize John 16:33.
* ❊ Memorize 1 Peter 5:7.
* ❊ Get regular exercise.
* ❊ Find a new hobby.
* ❊ If you have vacation time built up at work, take
  a half day off just to relax and do something fun.

* Go see a movie with a friend.
* Plan a girls' night out.
* Take a long, hot bubble bath.
* Read a good Christian novel.

Kick the Habits

"So if the Son sets you free, you will be free indeed."
JOHN 8:36 NIV

We are all sinners saved by the grace of God. Many of us, or our husbands, have come to the cross with a suitcase full of hurts and hang-ups. Many of these issues have affected our health and our marriage for years. How do you unpack those problems that are weighing you and your husband down? First you need to admit that you are powerless to change yourself (based on Romans 7:18 from the Celebrate Recovery program). Second, you must surrender your will completely to Christ. Third, you need some serious accountability in your life. You need to find someone who is spiritually mature—who will not judge, yet who will ask you the really tough questions.

I have some unhealthy habits in my life, Lord.
I surrender myself to You and know that only
You can help me change. Amen.

Action Point

Join a Celebrate Recovery program at your local church. Visit www.celebraterecovery.com to find a group near you. There are over ten thousand churches worldwide that host this program.

Scripture to Remember

Oh, what a miserable person I am! Who will free me
from this life that is dominated by sin and death?
Thank God! The answer is in Jesus Christ our Lord.
ROMANS 7:24–25 NLT

Checklist for Improvement:

* ❈ Seek the approval of God rather than your peers.
* ❈ Memorize John 5:41–42.
* ❈ Surround yourself with positive influences.
* ❈ Spend time with God each day, asking for His power and guidance to kick the bad habits in your life.

- ✽ Replace negative thoughts with scripture.
- ✽ Memorize Philippians 4:8.
- ✽ Acknowledge God in everything you do.
- ✽ Seek wisdom from God's Word on a daily basis.
- ✽ Journal your thoughts and feelings when you are struggling.

A Hug a Day

One person gives freely, yet gains even more.
PROVERBS 11:24 NIV

There are many health benefits to maintaining a happy marriage. Stress in marriage is often linked to illness. In a recent news study, psychologist Karen Grewen found that "each time we hug, we increase the level of oxytocin in the blood. This hormone is known as the bonding hormone because it triggers a 'caring' response in both men and women." Make it a point to welcome your spouse home from work each day with a lengthy hug, and you will both feel the stress of your day lessen. And you'll be improving the condition of your heart—and your marriage!

Thank You, Abba God, for creating the hug and
allowing it to reduce stress. Keep our marriage
healthy and happy. Amen.

Action Point

Give your husband at least a twenty-second hug as soon as you see him at the end of each workday.

Scripture to Remember

Be joyful. Grow to maturity. Encourage each other.
Live in harmony and peace. Then the God
of love and peace will be with you.
Greet each other with Christian love.
2 CORINTHIANS 13:11–12 NLT

Checklist for Improvement:

❋ Hugs are powerful and intimate. Avoid hugging men other than your husband unless it is a close relative. If it is unavoidable to hug another man in a certain situation, a side hug will do.

❋ Is physical touch yours or your husband's love language? Make sure you are showing love to your husband in the way that meets his needs. Be open and honest about your own needs.

* Hold hands and display affection with your husband daily.
* Give your husband a back massage.
* Run your fingers through your husband's hair, touch his face, and look into his eyes.
* Whenever you pass each other in the house or outside, give each other a squeeze or a love pat.
* Make it your goal to touch each other several times a day.
* Hold hands when you pray at dinner.
* Hug each other while you pray before bed.

Setting Goals

Stick with me, friends. Keep track of those you see running this same course, headed for this same goal.
PHILIPPIANS 3:17 MSG

The Bible tells us that we shouldn't run like a man running aimlessly. We should have a set purpose in mind, and this also applies to our health and our marriages. To keep your heart and marriage healthy, you need a plan. Carry out your goals with "purpose in every step" (1 Corinthians 9:26 NLT). Larry Elder says, "A goal without a plan is just a wish." Are you just wishing for a happy marriage and a healthy heart, or do you really plan to go after those objectives and achieve them? Begin setting goals so that you have something to aim for.

Father God, I want to do the best I can with all that You've given me, including my health and my marriage. Help me to succeed at these goals. Amen.

Action Point

1. Define your goals and write them down individually and as a couple.
2. Make a daily plan to attain these goals.
3. Give yourself a time limit to measure your success.

Scripture to Remember

So I run with purpose in every step. I am not just shadowboxing. I discipline my body like an athlete, training it to do what it should.
1 CORINTHIANS 9:26–27 NLT

Checklist for Improvement:

❋ Keep moving. People who fidget burn more calories throughout the day.
❋ Park at the back of the parking lot.
❋ Take the stairs instead of the elevator.

- Weigh yourself every morning to help yourself stay on track. If the scale depresses you, measure your success by how your clothes are fitting.
- Post your goals on the refrigerator.
- Go over your health goals with your doctor at your next checkup.
- Get rid of all the junk food in your home.
- Stretch before working out.

♥

I thank God each time I think about this day.
He has started something good in us
and we pledge our hearts today.
It is right for me to feel the way I do.
God took my hand and led me to you.

"I Hold You in My Heart," © 2001
by MariLee Parrish

♥

My Thoughts

Creating a Haven

~Improve Your Surroundings~

41

Queen of the Home

Who can find a virtuous and capable wife?
She is more precious than rubies.
PROVERBS 31:10 NLT

Your home should be a place where you, your husband, and your family can shut the door on the outside world and enjoy one another in peace and joy. You have the opportunity to be the queen of your home. We've all heard the saying that "If Mama ain't happy, ain't nobody happy." It is your responsibility to set the mood in your home. You get to choose if your home will be a place of peace and love, or chaos and strife.

Dear Lord, help me to take my responsibilities at
home very seriously. I want to be a wife who brings
good to my family all the days of my life. Amen.

Action Point

Take a mental inventory of your home environment. What do you like about your home atmosphere? What needs changing?

Scripture to Remember

Her husband can trust her, and she will greatly enrich his life. She brings him good, not harm, all the days of her life.
PROVERBS 31:11–12 NLT

Checklist for Improvement:

* ❊ Buy potted flowers and plants to improve the environment in your home.
* ❊ Research plants that clean the air, too.
* ❊ If you don't have a green thumb, find silk flowers that look real.
* ❊ Hang mirrors and add bright lamps to lighten up a dark room.
* ❊ Consider replacing worn carpet with hardwood floors and beautiful rugs.
* ❊ Change dark window coverings to something light and airy.

- ✽ Get rid of clutter and old knickknacks.
- ✽ Look online for some great interior designs that would work in your home. Re-create them economically, working within your budget.

The House

*She gets up before dawn to prepare breakfast
for her household and plan the day's work
for her servant girls.*
PROVERBS 31:15 NLT

The wife in Proverbs 31 seems like Wonder Woman, doesn't she? But don't forget that she had servant girls! So we'll just focus on doing the best we can and not striving for perfection. Most families like to come home to a clean, odor-free house at the end of a long day at school or work. Kicking your way through the door and stepping into a gooey pile of peanut butter and jelly just adds more stress after a chaotic day. If you set a timer every morning for three minutes before heading out the door and have the entire household pick or wipe up as much as they can in that three minutes, it will go a long way toward keeping household stress at bay.

*I'd like my home to feel more like a haven than a
headache, God. Please help me to get my family on
board as we strive to make our environment a little
more peaceful. Amen.*

Action Point

Create a cleaning schedule and a chore chart. Everyone in
your household can do something to help keep the house
clean.

Scripture to Remember

> *She is energetic and strong, a hard worker.*
> PROVERBS 31:17 NLT

Checklist for Improvement:

* List your cleaning priorities. Do you want the
  bedroom and the kitchen to always been clean?
  Focus on those areas first.
* Visit www.flylady.net to find simple ideas to
  keep your home organized.
* Do one load of laundry per day. Fold it while
  watching your favorite show.
* If you have young children, designate a room

or rooms for toys. Don't allow toys to clutter every room.

🌸 Decorate your house in a way that you enjoy. Don't worry about keeping up with the neighbors.

🌸 Strive for excellence, not perfection. Your house is meant to be lived in, not be an immaculate showplace for a magazine.

🌸 Create a daily chore list that will take you fifteen minutes or less each day.

🌸 Listen to worship music while you clean.

🌸 Do the most dreaded chores first, then the rest will be a breeze.

🌸 Clean light fixtures, air vents, window treatments, and outside windows on a monthly basis.

The Bedroom

Her hands are busy spinning thread, her fingers
twisting fiber. . . . She makes her own bedspreads.
PROVERBS 31:19, 22 NLT

Your bedroom should be a private haven just for you and your husband. Marriage lesson number one concerning your bedroom: Do *not* have a TV in your bedroom! Countless marriage counselors and relationship books will tell you the same. As much as it might hurt to remove it from your room, it must be done. If your husband resists this change, let him know that you'll replace the TV with romantic music so that you can spend more time being intimate. He'll probably have it out of the room within minutes. Marriage lesson number two: Remove all evidence of work from your bedroom. If you have your desk or a computer in your bedroom, find a new place for it. To transform your bedroom into a romantic haven, try and rearrange your room to feel more like a bed-and-breakfast. Dirty laundry and work papers strewn around will stifle romance quickly.

Prince of Peace, help us transform our bedroom into a place of rest, relaxation, and romance. Amen.

Action Point

Draw a diagram of your room. As a couple, decide how you can rearrange the area to feel more like a romantic getaway suite rather than a regular bedroom.

Scripture to Remember

She carefully watches everything in her household and suffers nothing from laziness.
PROVERBS 31:27 NLT

Checklist for Improvement:

❀ Saturday morning snuggles with your kids are okay, but don't allow your children to sleep in your bedroom on a regular basis. This can add stress and resentment in your marriage.

❀ Instead of allowing the kids to come in your bed when they are frightened or have a bad dream, offer to lie down beside them in their bed until they fall asleep.

❀ Keep romantic music on hand.

- ❋ Give your bedroom a new coat of paint.
- ❋ Purchase three-way lightbulbs for your lamps. Turn lights on the lowest setting to add warmth to your room.
- ❋ Put clean laundry away in closets or dressers and put dirty laundry in the hamper. Don't let it pile up on the floor or on your bed.
- ❋ Splurge on soft sheets, fluffy pillows, and comfortable bedding. You'll save in the long run by purchasing high-quality bedding materials.
- ❋ Place beautiful, inexpensive artwork on the walls.
- ❋ Make or purchase window décor to complement the color of the room.
- ❋ Place candles on the nightstand and around the room in groupings.

The Closet

She dresses in fine linen and purple gowns.
Her husband is well known at the city gates,
where he sits with the other civic leaders.
PROVERBS 31:22–23 NLT

If you have kids to clothe and babies to feed, your wardrobe is one of the last things to receive any attention. It's time to go through the closet. If you still have clothes that you wore in the eighties, it's time for a change. Get rid of anything you haven't worn in the last year. As wives, it's important that we wear clothing that our husbands appreciate. We want him to be attracted to us; and we don't want him to be embarrassed if we happen to run into his boss or coworkers at the grocery store. This is not to say that we need to be dressed to the hilt all the time, but it is important to take care of our appearance and avoid wearing old, grubby clothing unless the outing specifically calls for that.

*Help me to honor my husband in what I wear, Father
God. Provide us with some extra funds to add a few
new items to my wardrobe. Amen.*

Action Point

This could be the most difficult step for selfless women who
focus all of their time and attention on their family. You don't
have to break the bank, but it is okay to spend some money
on yourself every once in a while. If you're still feeling bad
about using money from the family budget on yourself, have
a garage sale to raise funds for a small new wardrobe. Purchase several classic, mix-and-match outfits that can be worn
throughout the seasons.

Scripture to Remember

*She is clothed with strength and dignity,
and she laughs without fear of the future.*
PROVERBS 31:25 NLT

Checklist for Improvement:

❋ Go through a current style magazine and try to re-create an outfit you like by shopping at a discount store or thrift shop.

❋ Ask for some wardrobe advice from a fashionable friend or family member.

❋ Purchase a few interchangeable, inexpensive accessories to go with your outfits.

❋ Organize a clothing swap among friends who are about the same size.

❋ Shop during sales and end-of-season clearances.

❋ Learn to sew. Make a few simple shirts to add to your wardrobe.

❋ Shop at factory outlets.

❋ Shop online using coupon codes.

❋ If you find a great deal on clothes in a larger size, calculate the cost to have the items altered. You might still save a bundle!

❋ Look in the papers for garage sales mentioning clothing. You may find several cute pieces to add to your collection.

The Kitchen

*She goes to inspect a field and buys it; with her
earnings she plants a vineyard.*
PROVERBS 31:16 NLT

The kitchen is often referred to as "the heart of the home."
Why? Because that's where families gather and real relationships take place. Sometimes a good meal can make all the
difference. Intimacy is cultivated over good food and conversation. If you aren't adept at cooking or baking, your marriage
and family relationships could benefit from a few cooking
classes. Even if your husband is the main chef of the house, he
would enjoy a night off once in a while. Creating a wonderful
meal is a gift that you can give your husband and your family
on a regular basis.

*Thank You, Lord, for the gift of a good meal.
Allow me to bless my husband and my family in this way.
Amen.*

Action Point

Take a local cooking class or rent a cooking video from your library. Try out a new recipe every week.

Scripture to Remember

> *She is like a merchant's ship,*
> *bringing her food from afar.*
> PROVERBS 31:14 NLT

Checklist for Improvement:

* Plant a small herb garden to set in your kitchen window.
* Cook together as a couple once a week.
* Make your husband's favorite meal on a regular basis.
* Keep your kitchen tidy. Nothing is less appetizing than a dirty, stinky kitchen.
* Keep lemon juice or a cleaner handy to keep smells out of the garbage disposal.
* Make more slow-cooker meals. The smells fill the house as the food is cooking, creating a warm and inviting atmosphere.

- ✻ Simmer a pot of cinnamon or potpourri in your kitchen.
- ✻ Pray before meals. Share something you're thankful for before eating.
- ✻ Eat slowly and enjoy each other. Talk about your day during dinner.
- ✻ Use fresh vegetables, fruits, and herbs whenever possible.

Financial Fun

She makes sure her dealings are profitable;
her lamp burns late into the night.
PROVERBS 31:18 NLT

Financial and *fun*. Can those words really show up next to each other? Financial stress can put a lot of strain on a marriage. If you're not getting the balance right, chances are finances will cause big problems in your marriage down the road. One person in the marriage is usually more financially savvy than the other. That person should take over the bulk of your financial situation, but both of you should share in the financial decisions and be aware of where the money goes in your family. If neither of you are that great at managing money, take a class together and get some help. You can treat your finances as a project to do together. Make paying the bills fun and turn "bill time" into something you can actually look forward to. Check out the ideas that follow.

Give us the wisdom to become better stewards of our money, Lord. Help us to remember that everything we have is Yours. Amen.

Action Point

Schedule a time on the calendar that coincides with your pay dates. Avoid Friday nights and weekends if you can. Schedule forty-five minutes to an hour to pay the bills, look over the finances, and discuss financial goals. Make your favorite dessert and be sure to stash away a few dollars for your "romance fund."

Scripture to Remember

> *God's blessing makes life rich;*
> *nothing we do can improve on God.*
> PROVERBS 10:22 MSG

Checklist for Improvement:

* ❀ Join a finance class at a local church.
* ❀ Visit www.debtproofliving.com for practical tips on improving your financial situation.
* ❀ Get on the same page when it comes to finances in your marriage. Commit to working

through things together.

🌸 Work to change your attitude about your finances. Pray for God's help in that area.

🌸 Begin saving for retirement.

🌸 Save for a fun anniversary vacation.

🌸 Always spend less than you earn.

🌸 Remember, money is just money. Don't obsess over it. It will never buy happiness.

🌸 Memorize Ecclesiastes 5:10.

Tithes and Blessings

*Each of you should give what you have decided in
your heart to give, not reluctantly or under
compulsion, for God loves a cheerful giver.*

2 CORINTHIANS 9:7 NIV

Are you and your husband experiencing financial blessing or are you having a hard time economically? In Matthew
19:24, Jesus tells us that "it is easier for a camel to go through
the eye of a needle than for someone who is rich to enter
the kingdom of God" (NIV). Why is that? Probably because
money has a lot to do with faith. The rich man didn't want
to trust God with his money. Do you trust God with your
money? Are you giving Him the first portion of your income?
Test Him in this. He tells us that we *should* test Him in this
(see Malachi 3:10)! See what happens if you live by faith with
your money. Start giving it away, and see how God blesses
your life and your marriage.

Heavenly Father, my faith is weak in this area.
Help me to give, and to live by faith. Amen.

Action Point

Start tithing every paycheck. Set aside a portion of your money to give to your local church. See if God makes your 90 percent go a lot further than your 100 percent ever did!

Scripture to Remember

"Bring the whole tithe into the storehouse, that there
may be food in my house. Test me in this," says the
Lord Almighty, "and see if I will not throw open the
floodgates of heaven and pour out so much blessing that
there will not be room enough to store it."
MALACHI 3:10 NIV

Checklist for Improvement:

* Begin collecting spare change. Give it to someone in need at the end of the year.
* Pick a Christian charity or mission and donate to it whenever you have the chance.
* Donate clothes, food, and toys to a local shelter several times a year.

- ❊ Hold a community garage sale. Donate the proceeds to charity.
- ❊ Instead of trading in your car, donate it to someone in need.
- ❊ Give away used laptops, electronics, and cell phones when upgrading.
- ❊ Leave better tips when you go out to eat.
- ❊ Try out this principal principle: Give 10 percent. Save 10 percent. Live off of 80 percent.

The Black Cloud

*Owe nothing to anyone—except for your obligation
to love one another.*
Romans 13:8 nlt

Unsecured debt is the black cloud that looms over your safe
haven and blocks the sunlight and color from your life. College loans, your mortgage, your cars—how can anyone live
without debt, you ask? Many debts can't be avoided. School
loans and mortgages are considered "investment debt," while
credit cards and lines of credit are considered unsecured or
"bad debt." Avoid bad debt at all costs. Dave Ramsey, the
founder of Financial Peace University, urges everyone to run
from debt with "gazelle intensity!" He also teaches to "live
like no one else, so later you can live like no one else." In other
words, scrimp, save, don't go out to eat, and don't splurge
until every bit of unsecured debt has been paid off. Then later
you can live—and give—like no one else.

*Help me to take my debt seriously, dear Lord. Forgive
me for my selfishness. Help me to do everything I can
to pay off my debts. Amen.*

Action Point

Make a plan to quickly repay your debt. List all of your debts,
their interest rates, and their due dates. Never miss a pay-
ment, and, if possible, pay more than the minimum due.
Consider selling some rarely used, high-dollar items to help
pay down your debt.

Scripture to Remember

> *A prudent person foresees danger
> and takes precautions. The simpleton goes
> blindly on and suffers the consequences.*
> PROVERBS 27:12 NLT

Checklist for Improvement:

* ❋ Take on an extra job until some high-interest-
  rate debts are paid.
* ❋ Visit www.ChristianMomsBusinessResource.
  com to learn ways to earn extra money or find a
  part-time job from home.

- ✼ Always live below your means.
- ✼ Look for ways to slash spending. Use the savings to make higher debt payments.
- ✼ Use coupons. Go to www.couponmom.com. They help you match coupons with the sales ads in your local store, saving you a significant amount of money on everyday groceries.
- ✼ Destroy all of your credit cards and start an emergency fund to replace the credit cards.
- ✼ Apply any extra cash—monetary birthday gifts, refunds, etc.—to debt.
- ✼ Cancel magazine and paper subscriptions. Read them online instead.
- ✼ Switch your TV service to only the basic stations. E-mail more. Talk on the phone less.
- ✼ Use your savings to pay down debt.

Open Your Doors

She extends a helping hand to the poor and opens
her arms to the needy. She has no fear of winter for
her household, for everyone has warm clothes.
PROVERBS 31:20–21 NLT

If you have a roof over your head, you are more fortunate than 35 percent of the population in the United States alone. Most of us have been blessed beyond measure. If you have been creating a haven and a beautiful home for your family, ask the Lord to show you how you can use it as a ministry. This doesn't mean that you allow strangers into your house or that you have an open-door policy any time day or night. But could you open your home to a small group or Bible study? Could you use your kitchen to make meals for a needy family or a mother who's just had a baby? Pray about ways to open your doors to bless others. Serving God and serving others will strengthen your marriage and your family like nothing else.

*Thank You for how You've blessed us, Jesus. Show us
ways to use what You've given us to bless others. Amen.*

Action Point

Check with the secretary or leadership staff at your church.
Find out if a Bible study or ministry of some sort needs a
home, then offer yours.

Scripture to Remember

> *For I testify that they gave as much as they were able,
> and even beyond their ability.*
> 2 CORINTHIANS 8:3 NIV

Checklist for Improvement:

* Host a barbecue. Ask everyone to bring a
  canned good as their entrance fee to give away
  to a local homeless shelter.
* Make a list of the people you know who are
  having surgery or women who are having a
  baby in the coming months. Call them up and
  offer to bring over meals.
* Plan a fall party for neighborhood kids. Carve
  pumpkins, sing songs, and share God's love

however you can.

* As a family, create handmade cards for people who are ill or in the hospital.

* Invite the Sunday school kids over for a picnic.

* Offer to share a talent or skill that you have: Bake a special cake, teach a cooking class, cut hair, etc.

* Do you have a hot tub, a large pond, or a pool? Contact members of your church staff and offer to let them use it for baptisms.

* Plant a garden and give the abundance to those around you who would be blessed by it.

The Heart of It All

Her husband praises her: "There are many virtuous and capable women in the world, but you surpass them all!"
PROVERBS 31:28–29 NLT

Wouldn't it be great to have a happy marriage? Wouldn't you love it if your husband not only said—but truly believed—that out of all the women in the world, you surpass them all? Proverbs 31 gives us a great outline for how to accomplish this. The Bible is very clear that it's not about outward beauty or charm; it's all about the heart. It's the woman who honors the Lord in her daily life who will be praised by her husband and children. As you walk with God throughout life, listen to His promptings and the many ways that He speaks to you. Then follow through!

God in heaven, thank You for giving us words of wisdom and examples to model our life after. Allow me to honor You in all that I do. Amen.

Action Point

Journal the various ways that God speaks to you today. When do you hear Him most clearly?

Scripture to Remember

> *Charm is deceptive, and beauty does not last;*
> *but a woman who fears the Lord will be greatly praised.*
> PROVERBS 31:30 NLT

Checklist for Improvement:

* Memorize John 10:27.
* Practice being still. Be still before God and learn to recognize His still, small voice.
* Start a journal. Record the many ways that God is working in your life.
* Spend a full hour with God on a regular basis. Use the suggestions that follow to stay on track.
* Read several Psalms and pray them back to God.
* Confess your sins to the Lord and ask forgiveness.
* Count your blessings and thank God for each one.

- ✿ Praise God for who He is.
- ✿ Turn on some worship music and sing along.
- ✿ Pray for your husband, kids, extended family, leaders, and unsaved friends/family in your life.

*Nothing can bring a real sense of security
into the home except true love.*

Billy Graham

My Thoughts

Conclusion

$\mathcal{E}$very married couple knows that marriage is hard work. As women, God calls us to love our husbands—no matter what. Only when you abide in Christ are you able to fully love each other as God loves. With Christ as the center of your home, you have God's power to transform your home and marriage into one that is joyful, loving, and honoring to Him.

Father, I pray that we would seek You above all else and that You would fill our hearts and home with Your love. I pray for my husband, that he would fully commit his life to You and that I would support and encourage him daily. Be the center of our marriage. In Jesus' name, amen.

Additional Scriptures to Remember

Comfort

*The Lord is a refuge for the oppressed,
a stronghold in times of trouble.*
PSALM 9:9 NIV

*Wait for the Lord; be strong and take heart
and wait for the Lord.*
PSALM 27:14 NIV

*God is our refuge and strength,
an ever-present help in trouble.*
PSALM 46:1 NIV

*Though I walk in the midst of trouble, you preserve my life.
You stretch out your hand against the anger of my foes,
with your right hand you save me.*
PSALM 138:7 NIV

Communication

Let the wise listen and add to their learning,
and let the discerning get guidance.
PROVERBS 1:5 NIV

Light in a messenger's eyes brings joy to the heart, and good
news gives health to the bones. Whoever heeds life-giving
correction will be at home among the wise.
PROVERBS 15:30–31 NIV

My child, listen and be wise:
Keep your heart on the right course.
PROVERBS 23:19 NLT

Do not let any unwholesome talk come out of your mouths,
but only what is helpful for building others up according
to their needs, that it may benefit those who listen.
EPHESIANS 4:29 NIV

Everyone should be quick to listen,
slow to speak and slow to become angry.
JAMES 1:19 NIV

Encouragement

*"Have I not commanded you? Be strong and courageous.
Do not be afraid; do not be discouraged, for the Lord
your God will be with you wherever you go."*
JOSHUA 1:9 NIV

*Jesus replied, "What is impossible with
man is possible with God."*
LUKE 18:27 NIV

*"What do you mean, 'If I can'?" Jesus asked.
"Anything is possible if a person believes."*
MARK 9:23 NLT

*And we know that in all things God works for the good of those
who love him, who have been called according to his purpose.*
ROMANS 8:28 NIV

*What, then, shall we say in response to these things?
If God is for us, who can be against us?*
ROMANS 8:31 NIV

Faith

*"Truly I tell you, if you have faith as small as a mustard seed,
you can say to this mountain, 'Move from here to there'
and it will move. Nothing will be impossible for you."*
MATTHEW 17:20 NIV

*Yet to all who did receive him, to those who believed in
his name, he gave the right to become children of God.*
JOHN 1:12 NIV

*Jesus said to her, "I am the resurrection and the life.
The one who believes in me will live, even though they die."*
JOHN 11:25 NIV

*If anyone acknowledges that Jesus is the Son of God,
God lives in them and they in God.*
1 JOHN 4:15 NIV

Finances

Those who trust in their riches will fall,
but the righteous will thrive like a green leaf.
PROVERBS 11:28 NIV

For the love of money is a root of all kinds of evil.
Some people, eager for money, have wandered from
the faith and pierced themselves with many griefs.
1 TIMOTHY 6:10 NIV

Command those who are rich in this present world
not to be arrogant nor to put their hope in wealth, which is
so uncertain, but to put their hope in God, who richly provides
us with everything for our enjoyment. Command them to
do good, to be rich in good deeds, and to be generous and
willing to share. In this way they will lay up treasure for
themselves as a firm foundation for the coming age,
so that they may take hold of the life that is truly life.
1 TIMOTHY 6:17–19 NIV

Forgiveness

Do not say, "I'll pay you back for this wrong!"
Wait for the Lord, and he will avenge you.
PROVERBS 20:22 NIV

"For if you forgive other people when they sin against you,
your heavenly Father will also forgive you."
MATTHEW 6:14 NIV

"And when you stand praying, if you hold anything
against anyone, forgive them, so that your Father
in heaven may forgive you your sins."
MARK 11:25 NIV

"Be merciful, just as your Father is merciful."
LUKE 6:36 NIV

God's Love

*Love the Lord your God with all your heart and
with all your soul and with all your strength.*
DEUTERONOMY 6:5 NIV

*By day the Lord directs his love, at night his song
is with me—a prayer to the God of my life.*
PSALM 42:8 NIV

*The Lord is compassionate and gracious,
slow to anger, abounding in love.*
PSALM 103:8 NIV

*"For God so loved the world that he gave his one and only Son,
that whoever believes in him shall not perish but have eternal
life. For God did not send his Son into the world to condemn
the world, but to save the world through him."*
JOHN 3:16–17 NIV

Whoever does not love does not know God, because God is love.
1 JOHN 4:8 NIV

Hope

Be strong and take heart, all you who hope in the Lord.
PSALM 31:24 NIV

But the eyes of the Lord are on those who fear him,
on those whose hope is in his unfailing love.
PSALM 33:18 NIV

Yes, my soul, find rest in God; my hope comes from him.
PSALM 62:5 NIV

Be joyful in hope, patient in affliction, faithful in prayer.
ROMANS 12:12 NIV

So that, having been justified by his grace, we might become
heirs having the hope of eternal life.
TITUS 3:7 NIV

Love & Marriage

*Wives, submit yourselves to your husbands,
as is fitting in the Lord.*
COLOSSIANS 3:18 NIV

Husbands, love your wives and do not be harsh with them.
COLOSSIANS 3:19 NIV

*The same goes for you husbands: Be good husbands
to your wives. Honor them, delight in them. As women
they lack some of your advantages. But in the new life of God's
grace, you're equals. Treat your wives, then, as equals
so your prayers don't run aground.*
1 PETER 3:7 MSG

*Dear children, let us not love with words
or speech but with actions and in truth.*
1 JOHN 3:18 NIV

*And this is his command: to believe in the name of his Son,
Jesus Christ, and to love one another as he commanded us.*
1 JOHN 3:23 NIV

Scripture Index